i explore

WHAT'S INSIDE?

Discover more about amazing space!

The Universe

Earth & the Moon

Space exploration

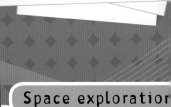

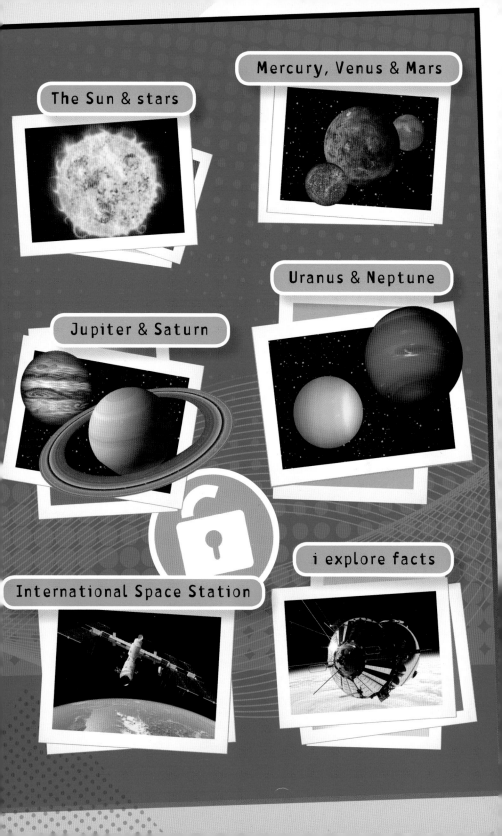

The Sun & stars

Mercury, Venus & Mars

Uranus & Neptune

Jupiter & Saturn

International Space Station

i explore facts

THE UNIVERSE

The Universe is the name we give to everything that exists, including all of the stars, planets, and galaxies. Many scientists believe it began in a giant explosion called the Big Bang!

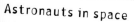

Astronauts in space

i discover

The Universe contains billions of galaxies. A galaxy is a group of stars, dust, and gas, held together by an invisible force called gravity. This force pulls objects together and stops them from flying off into space! There is not enough gravity to hold astronauts down in space – this is why they look like they are floating!

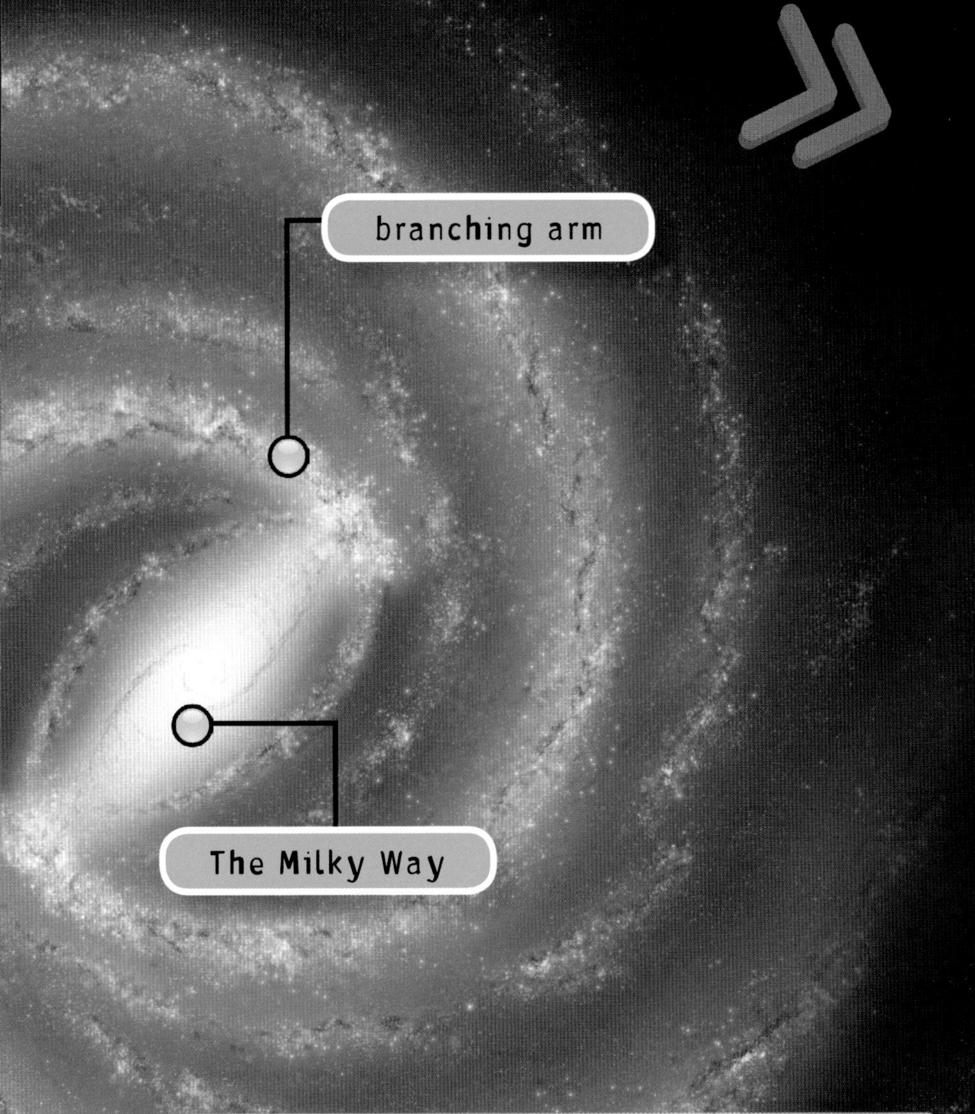

branching arm

The Milky Way

→ i learn ✕

Galaxies come in different shapes. We live in a galaxy called the Milky Way. It is called a spiral-shaped galaxy because the arms that branch out from its center make it look like a spiral.

The Milky Way seen from Earth

The Solar System

« »

⌂ | i facts | 🔍

The Solar System is the name we give to our Sun and the planets, moons, comets, and asteroids that circle around it.

The Milky Way has about 200 thousand, million stars.

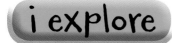
THE SUN AND STARS

The Sun is the star in the middle of our Solar System. It is a huge ball of extremely hot gas. Without the Sun, there would be no life on Earth.

→ i learn

A star can live for millions of years. The Sun is actually a medium-sized star – it will keep giving us heat and light for another five thousand, million years!

The Sun's gravity makes all the planets in our Solar System travel in circular paths around it. These paths are called orbits. Earth takes one year to complete an orbit around the Sun.

Planets in our Solar System in orbit

i fact

Shooting stars look like flashes of light flying across the sky. They are made up of pieces of ice and rock called meteors.

Shooting star

MERCURY, VENUS, and MARS

Venus

»

The inner Solar System is made up of four planets – Mercury, Venus, Earth, and Mars – and the asteroid belt!

Mercury

i facts

When Mercury passes between Earth and the Sun, we see it as a black dot against the Sun's surface. This is called a transit.

From Earth, Venus looks very bright. This is because its clouds reflect light from the Sun.

Mars is nicknamed the Red Planet. It gets its reddish-brown color from the dust, sand, and rocks on its surface.

Mars

i discover

An asteroid is a large piece of rock or metal that is left over from the time when the planets were forming. Most asteroids can be found in orbit between Mars and Jupiter. This area is called the asteroid belt.

Asteroid belt

atmosphere

EARTH AND THE MOON

Earth has the perfect combination of temperature, atmosphere, and water for us to live. So far, humans have only set foot on Earth and the Moon.

i learn

Objects that orbit a planet or star are called satellites. The Moon is a satellite that orbits Earth. It shines in the night sky because it reflects the light of the Sun.

The Moon orbiting Earth

Earth

Crater on the Moon

❌

💡 i discover

An atmosphere is a layer of gas that surrounds a planet – Earth's atmosphere makes up the air that we breathe. When a meteor enters Earth's atmosphere, it usually burns up before it hits the ground. The Moon has no atmosphere, so meteors often hit its surface, causing craters.

Moon

crater

15

Earth seen from space

i facts

i Three-quarters of Earth's surface is covered in water.

The first men to walk on the Moon were Neil Armstrong and Buzz Aldrin in 1969.

Buzz Aldrin on the Moon

JUPITER AND SATURN

Jupiter and Saturn are made mostly of gas. They are the two largest planets in the Solar System, and scientists call them the gas giants!

Saturn

i discover

Saturn's rings are made up of millions of pieces of ice, which are thought to be pieces of an old moon that smashed apart many years ago.

Pieces of ice from Saturn's rings

Great Red Spot

Jupiter is covered in swirling gas clouds, so it looks different every day. The largest gas cloud is called the Great Red Spot. This is a storm that is bigger than Earth and has lasted for hundreds of years.

Jupiter

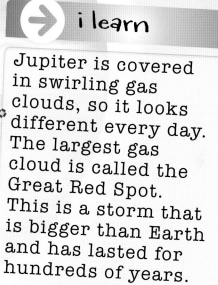

Jupiter and Ganymede

i facts

i Jupiter's moon, Ganymede, is the biggest moon in the Solar System.

Saturn's rings are long enough to circle Earth over 44 times!

URANUS AND NEPTUNE

Uranus and Neptune are the two planets farthest away from the Sun. A gas called methane in the planets' atmospheres gives them their blue-green colors.

Uranus

poles

i learn

Uranus is at a different angle to all the other planets – its poles look as though they are on its sides. Scientists think that Uranus may have collided with another planet causing it to lean this way.

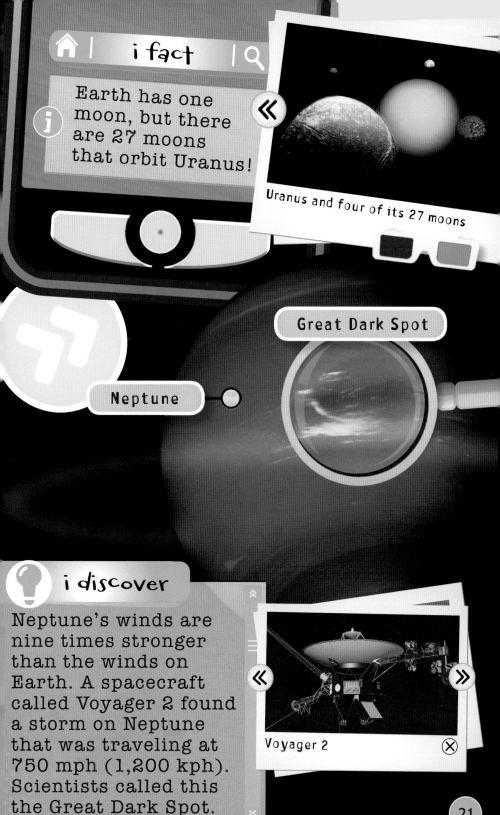

🏠 | i fact | 🔍

ⓘ Earth has one moon, but there are 27 moons that orbit Uranus!

«

Uranus and four of its 27 moons

Great Dark Spot

Neptune ○

💡 i discover

Neptune's winds are nine times stronger than the winds on Earth. A spacecraft called Voyager 2 found a storm on Neptune that was traveling at 750 mph (1,200 kph). Scientists called this the Great Dark Spot.

« »

Voyager 2

ⓧ

SPACE EXPLORATION

The first man in space was a Russian named Yuri Gagarin who orbited Earth in 1961. Since then, humans have been exploring space in new and amazing ways!

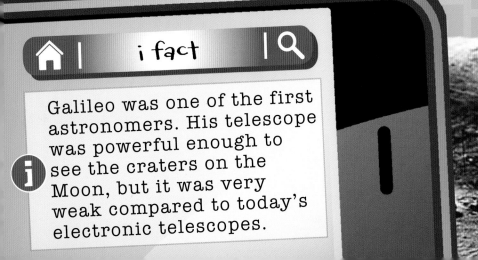

🏠 | i fact | 🔍

Galileo was one of the first astronomers. His telescope was powerful enough to see the craters on the Moon, but it was very weak compared to today's electronic telescopes.

helmet

One of the most powerful telescopes today is the Hubble telescope, which orbits Earth. It has taken photos of the most distant galaxies in the Universe!

The Hubble telescope

visor

spacesuit

i learn

When astronauts are in space, they wear a spacesuit that protects them from the cold and provides air for them to breathe. A thin layer of gold on the helmet's visor ensures that the Sun's rays do not harm the astronaut's eyes.

The Spirit and Opportunity rovers were machines that landed on Mars in 2004. They sent vital information back to Earth, proving that Mars once had water.

INTERNATIONAL SPACE STATION

The International Space Station is a spacecraft that orbits Earth. Up to six people can live there at a time.

→ i learn

On the space station, astronauts observe Earth and space. Astronauts also complete spacewalks, when they leave the space station to carry out experiments or repairs in space!

The space station is powered by four sets of solar panels, which together are the size of 15 tennis courts!

The space station has an observation deck called the Cupola. This is where astronauts watch the work happening outside the spacecraft.

The Cupola

solar panel

27

astronaut

The space station is home to Robonaut 2 – a test robot that looks and moves a little like a human! Scientists hope it is the first step towards creating robots that can help people in space and on Earth.

Robonaut 2

The first living thing to travel into space was a dog! Laika the dog traveled in a spacecraft called Sputnik II, on a mission to find out whether living things could survive space travel.

If somebody shouted at you in space, you wouldn't be able to hear them – even if they shouted in your ear! This is because there's no air to carry the sound.

The largest galaxy we know of contains more than 100 million, million stars!

If you could find a swimming pool big enough to fit Saturn, it would float on water!

Mercury rotates on its axis much more slowly than Earth, which means that one day on Mercury would last 59 days on Earth!

You should never look right at the Sun – it will damage your eyes.